# Dwayne's Rain

By Pamela Rushby

Illustrated by James Hart

**Pearson Australia**
(a division of Pearson Australia Group Pty Ltd)
707 Collins Street, Melbourne, Victoria 3008
PO Box 23360, Melbourne, Victoria 8012
www.pearson.com.au


First published 2012 by Pearson Australia
2019 2018 2017 2016
10 9 8 7 6 5 4 3

Publisher: Sabine Bolick
Project Editor: Suzy Freeman
Editor: Kerry Nagle
Designer: Jennifer Johnston
Copyright & Pictures Editor: Marg Barber
Illustrator: James Hart
Printed and bound in Australia by Pegasus Media & Logistics

ISBN 978 1 4425 3774 3

Pearson Australia Group Pty Ltd ABN 40 004 245 943

# Contents

Chapter 1

# Earning Money

**If you wanted to earn** some money, what would you do? Wash people's cars? Walk dogs? Weed gardens?

There are hundreds of ways that kids can earn money. And my brother, Dwayne, has tried most of them. He's always having "bright" ideas about how to make some extra cash. And often, he'll have me right up to my neck in them, too.

"Ben," he'll say. "Ben, little brother. I've got this **idea**."

Sometimes, his ideas work.

A lot of times, they don't.

Dwayne has had **ideas** like delivering newspapers. That worked fine, until I discovered that Dwayne is not a morning person. It took me longer to wake him up every morning than it took us to deliver the newspapers.

Then he had an idea about walking dogs. That worked fine, too, until Dwayne agreed to walk Mrs Hudson's Twinky. Twinky is a Great Dane and the size of a pony. We didn't walk Twinky, Twinky walked us. He dragged us along behind him as he did laps of the park.

Terrified dogs and joggers scattered around us, until Twinky decided he'd had enough. And so had we.

Next was the garage sale. Dwayne had this idea to sell some old toys and games that we didn't play with any more. That seemed like an excellent idea. It was a complete mystery to us how Dad's golf clubs somehow got involved and disappeared forever.

And there was the time Dwayne had an idea about doing face-painting at Cindy Cho's birthday party. The faces we created were very artistic. And, as it happened, we had a lot of time to admire them, because unfortunately the paint we used wasn't the sort that comes off easily. It had to wear off. The parents were not happy.

And then there was the time that Dwayne thought we could go busking in the mall in town, him on his trumpet and me on my school recorder. Well, enough said about that one.

Now you have some idea about Dwayne's **ideas**. So, whenever Dwayne says "Ben, I've got this idea about earning some money", I've learned to be very, very cautious.

But this time, even I thought Dwayne was on to a winner.

Here is what happened …

Chapter 2

# The Drought

**It hadn't rained** for ages in the town where we live. Not just for a few weeks—it hadn't rained for months and months. The grass was dry and brown. Trees were drooping. The water level in the dams was low, so low that the council started putting water restrictions in place. We were in a **drought**.

We were being asked to take short showers, and not to use the washing machine every day. We could only water our gardens with a hose once a week.

The drought went on. The water level in the dams sank even lower. On the local news, we were asked to be very careful with the water we used. We were told that, from now on, we couldn't water our gardens with a hose at all. Hoses used too much water.

"We know gardens are very important to people," said the newsreader.

"So, to help keep your garden growing until we get rain again, you can collect the rinse water from the washing machine, and use buckets and watering cans to pour that water onto the garden. If you use special washing powder, it won't hurt the plants."

We all listened. We knew this was important. We were happy to help by watering our gardens with buckets and watering cans. What we didn't know was what hard work this was actually going to be.

A couple of days later, Mum asked Dwayne and me to help her with the watering. She'd saved the rinse water from the wash in the laundry tub. Now we needed to fill buckets and carry them out and empty them onto the garden.

It didn't take long to find out that a bucket full of water is amazingly heavy. It's also very **sloshy**—no matter how careful you are, it always seems to spill out of the bucket as you carry it.

We left puddles all the way from the laundry to the back door and down the back steps. Our arms were aching by the time we'd finished and our shorts were soaked. But at least the garden had been watered.

I was just pouring the last bucket onto Mum's pots of mint and parsley, when I heard a weird sound. It came from over the fence, from next door.

It sounded like something grunting and gasping. Like a wild animal? Surely Mrs Pappas didn't have a wild animal in her backyard!

Mrs Pappas is our next-door neighbour. She's old and lives by herself. She's a very keen gardener, with flowers in her front yard and an amazing vegie garden in her backyard. She grows tomatoes, beans, carrots, zucchini and pumpkin. She also has herbs like rosemary, basil, oregano and chives. She often gives us vegies, and the ones she grows taste heaps better than the ones Mum buys from the supermarket.

I went to the fence and stretched up to have a look over.

It wasn't an animal that was making those noises. It was Mrs Pappas, **lugging** a bucket of water to her vegie garden.

She was puffing and panting and groaning, and her face was red and her arms were trembling. While I watched, she stopped and put her hand up to her head for a second, as if she was feeling dizzy. And then she staggered and fell, and the water went everywhere.

"Ohmigosh!" I shouted. "Mum! Dad!"

Chapter 3

# Dwayne's Idea

**Mum, Dad, Dwayne and I** ran next door. Mum sat Mrs Pappas on a chair and Dad got her a glass of water. We all watched her worriedly as she sipped it.

"Are you all right?" Mum asked.

Mrs Pappas nodded. "I'm all right," she said, when she could talk. "But it looks like watering the garden this way is just too much for me. I simply can't manage these buckets. I can't do it." She looked at her garden. "My garden will die," she said sadly.

Mum gave Dwayne and me a look. Dwayne and I looked at each other. We knew it was hard work, carrying water, but still …

"We'll water your garden for you, Mrs Pappas," we said.

Mrs Pappas said she couldn't possibly let us, and then she said she'd pay us. Dwayne and I kept saying we were happy to help and we didn't want payment because she gave us vegies all the time.

Finally it was settled. We finished watering her garden and she gave us some tomatoes, basil and rosemary, and Mum turned them into a spaghetti sauce.

Dwayne was very quiet at dinner. Mum asked him something and he didn't answer. She asked again, louder.

Dwayne jumped and said, "Sorry, Mum. I was just thinking."

After dinner, Dwayne turned on the computer in the family room. I thought he was going to play a game—he was up to Level 4 on Dragons of Doom—but when I walked past, I saw he was working on something quite different.

I peered at the computer. There were a lot of big, coloured letters on the screen.

"What's that?" I asked.

Dwayne turned around. "Ben, little brother," he said. "Ben, I've got this fantastic **idea**."

I should have turned and run right then. I looked at the screen instead. The big, coloured letters were a flyer. It said:

**NO RAIN?**
**CALL DWAYNE!**
**I'LL MAKE IT RAIN ON YOUR PATCH!**

"Huh?" I said.

"Gardens," said Dwayne. "Water. We can water people's gardens, like we're doing for Mrs Pappas. But," he paused and grinned, "for other people, we don't do it for free. We charge them to water their gardens."

I wasn't sure about this. My arms were still aching from carrying buckets of water.

"It's hard work, watering with buckets and cans," I said.

Dwayne looked thoughtful. "Yes," he said at last. "Yes, it is. But hey, we'll be getting **paid** for it!"

I thought for a while. It sounded all right. It sounded as if it might work. "Okay," I said. "Count me in."

"Anyway," I thought, "Dwayne probably won't get many calls. Most people like to water their own gardens. There won't be much work involved. It will be all right."

Boy, was I wrong.

Chapter 4

# Dwayne's Next Idea

**Dwayne printed a lot of copies** of his flyer and we dropped them into letterboxes near home.

Some people were out in their garden when we went by. If someone was carrying a bucket of water, Dwayne put the flyer right into their hands and told them what we were doing.

A woman was trying to water a garden bed full of bright flowers around her letterbox while keeping an eye on her two-year-old twins.

"These snapdragons have only just started to flower," she told us. "I don't want to lose them, but it's not easy watching the twins and watering the garden at the same time." She looked over at the twins.

While she had been talking to us, the little girl had found a **puddle**. She was sitting in it and rubbing mud into her hair. The little boy had dug a worm out of the garden. He was about to eat it.

The woman dived at him and took the worm away. The little boy howled.

"Well," said the woman, "I think I'll be calling you!"

"You'll water my garden, eh?" an old man said. He had roses all along his front fence—dozens of them. The water from the bucket he had just emptied hadn't gone very far. I could see he was working out just how many buckets he'd have to carry to water every rose bush.

"That's not a bad idea. Let me think about it—but I'll probably be calling you."

It all looked very promising.

The first evening after we'd delivered the flyers, Dwayne waited by the phone **hopefully** for hours. There were no calls. And there were no calls the second day, either.

"Well, that's the end of that idea," I thought.

But then, on the third day, Dwayne got three calls. Three people wanted us

to water their gardens! Dwayne smiled. The next day, there were four more calls. Dwayne was really **happy**. Over the weekend, there were even more calls. Dwayne was thrilled. But then, the calls kept coming and coming and coming. Dwayne stopped being happy and started being **concerned**.

"We just can't do it!" he said to me. "We can't water all these gardens! There are only so many hours in the day."

I shrugged my shoulders. "So we don't do them all," I said. "You'll just have to tell anyone else who phones that we're fully booked."

I could see Dwayne hated to do that. "There must be a way," he frowned.

"Not unless you can **clone** us," I said. "Or not unless you can lay your hands on a bunch of Oompa-Loompas." (We were reading *Charlie and the Chocolate Factory* at school.) I laughed. It was a joke.

But Dwayne didn't laugh. He stared at me. "Clones, eh? Oompa-Loompas, eh?" he said. "Now there's an idea!"

I thought he was kidding. But he wasn't.

The next afternoon, a lot of kids came over to our house. They all wanted to see Dwayne. I sent them in to the family room. One by one they went in, and one by one they came out. They weren't there long enough to be playing Dragons of Doom or anything else, and there were so many of them. I couldn't stand it. I had to find out what was happening.

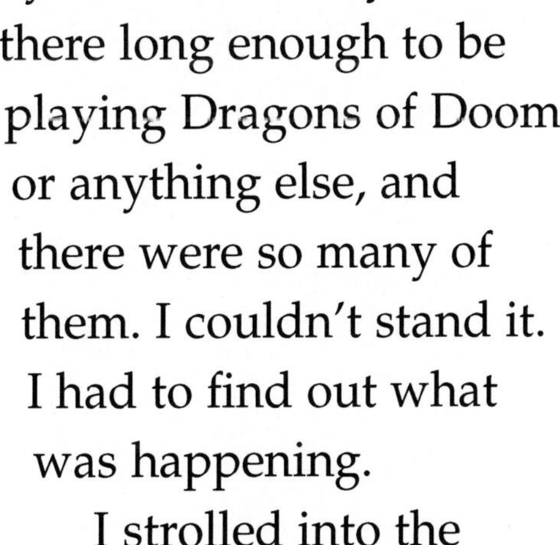

I strolled into the family room. There was a line of kids waiting in a queue. Dwayne was sitting at our picnic table, and he had an exercise book and some slips of paper.

"Now, your name is?" Dwayne was asking the girl standing in front of him.

"Mandy," the girl said.

"And where do you live?'

"I'm in Lawson Street," Mandy said.

Dwayne looked at his book. "Right, I've got two gardens in Lawson Street and one in Paterson Street. That's not far from you, is it?"

"No, it's the next street," Mandy said.

"So that's three gardens you could **water**, Mandy. Do you want to do that?" Dwayne looked at her closely.

She wasn't a very big girl. "*Could* you do that?" he asked. "I mean, buckets of water are heavy."

"I can do it," Mandy said. "I'm strong. I do karate." She looked Dwayne up and down thoughtfully. "I could probably throw you. Do you want me to try?"

"Er, no," Dwayne said. "No, that won't be necessary." He wrote on a slip of paper. "Here are the addresses you'll be doing," he said, handing it to her. "I'll pay you after you've watered three gardens."

"How much do I get paid?" Mandy wanted to know.

Dwayne told her. His answer surprised me, because I knew it was less than Dwayne was charging the owners of the gardens for doing the watering. Not a lot less, but it was still less. I didn't understand it but it was not the time to ask Dwayne about it, as he still had a queue of kids waiting to see him.

I went outside and waited until the last kid had left. Then I went back to the family room. Dwayne was tidying up his notebook and bits of paper.

"What's going on?" I wanted to know. "Who were all those kids and what were they doing here?"

"They're our workforce," said Dwayne. I must have looked blank, because he went on.

"Our **clones**. You know! Our Oompa-Loompas! These kids are watering all the gardens that we won't have time to do ourselves."

"Oh, right," I said. I thought about that. "Well, it's nice of you to pass the work on to them."

"Well," said Dwayne, "it's not exactly passing it on. Actually, I get something out of it too."

"And what's that?"

"The people who want their gardens watered pay me, right? And I pay the kids who are doing the work. But I pay them a bit less than I'm actually getting. The difference is what I get."

That was exactly what I'd thought was going on, but I'd wanted Dwayne to explain it because it was bothering me.

"Is that **fair**?" I asked. "I mean, they're doing the work!"

"Sure it's fair," said Dwayne. "After all, I found them the work."

"Oh," I said.

Chapter 5

# Is It Fair?

**I thought about it,** but it still didn't seem quite right to me. I went to water Mrs Pappas's garden, and thought about it some more. Mrs Pappas was very happy her garden wasn't going to dry up, and gave me a huge pumpkin.

I was staggering home with it just as Dad drove up and parked his truck in the driveway. Dad's a plumber. His truck has **GOT A DRIP? CALL RICK!** painted on the side.

He climbed out, pressing numbers on his mobile.

"Hello, Charlie," he said. "Did you manage to fit in that job I rang you about? You did? Great! What was the problem?" He went into a lot of technical, plumbing-type talk with Charlie, who is one of the guys who works for Dad.

"Okay," Dad said at last. "Good work! See you tomorrow." Dad switched off his mobile and looked at me and my pumpkin.

"Wow! Look at the size of that!" Dad said. "How about we make pumpkin soup for dinner?"

"Okay."

While Dad and I cut up the pumpkin and **zapped** it in the microwave, I thought about Dwayne, the kids and the work they were doing. I also thought about what they were being paid.

After a while, Dad stopped and looked at me. "You're very quiet, Ben. Anything the matter?"

"Dad, can I ask you something?" I said.

"Sure." He grinned at me.

"It's like this," I began, and I told him all about it.

"I see," Dad said, when I'd finished. He dropped pieces of cooked pumpkin into the blender and **whizzed** them into a pulp. "Well, I can answer that. It's the way a lot of businesses work. Someone has a great idea—"

"Like Dwayne did," I said.

"And lots of people want to use the service they're offering—"

"Like Dwayne's garden watering."

"And there's so much demand they can't do it all, so they pay other people to do the actual work. They pay the workers a bit less than they're charging the customer and they keep the difference."

"And that's okay?" I asked.

"Yes, it's quite okay. Because they had the great **idea** and they've done all the work of finding the clients." Dad added some chicken stock to the pumpkin pulp.

"It's the same in my plumbing business," he went on. "People ring me up to get work done, but when I can't do all the work myself, I employ people like Charlie to handle some of the jobs for me."

"And you pay Charlie a bit less than you charge your clients?" I asked.

"That's the way it works," Dad said.

"I see," I said. I was relieved that Dwayne wasn't doing anything wrong. "I guess that's fair enough, then."

Soon, Dwayne had kids all over town working for him. The clients were happy because their gardens were being watered. The kids were happy because they were being paid for their work.

And Dwayne was absolutely **thrilled**. He was making a lot of money. He had plans for a new bike. And maybe, he said, if things kept going well, he'd be able to take all of us away to the beach for a weekend.

Everyone seemed to be happy.

And then ... everything went wrong.

Chapter 6

# The Rain

**It started to rain.** But it didn't just rain. It poured.

It rained for days. Water ran down roofs and cascaded over overflowing gutters. Water **gurgled** down the streets and poured into storm drains. The drains emptied into creeks. The creeks rose and rose and overflowed. The dams were full. Every garden in town was completely soaked.

And Dwayne was out of work.

A woman on TV talked about how wonderful it was that the drought had ended. She thanked everyone for being so careful with water during the drought.

Dwayne wasn't watching TV. He was standing by the window with his hands in his pockets, looking at the rain **streaming** down the glass.

"Isn't it great?" I said. "Now people won't have to carry buckets."

Dwayne turned around and looked at me. Then he turned back and looked out the window again.

"Oh," I said.

I joined him at the window. I really felt sorry for Dwayne. It had been such a great idea to water people's gardens for them. But now it was over. There'd be no new bike or weekend at the beach.

I put my hands in my pockets too, and we stared out at the grey day. Grey sky. Heavy rain **hammering** down. Our roof gutters were blocked with leaves and overflowed with water. The front yard had a sheet of water covering it. Water ran down the road, pouring over the drains. Water flooded people's driveways. Water swamped garden beds and drowned plants.

Some of the water had started to flood garages. There was so much water!

"Those roof gutters and drains really need cleaning out," I said.

Dwayne turned around slowly and looked at me. "Say that again," he said.

"What?" I said. "That the gutters and drains need clearing?"

"Ben, little brother," said Dwayne. "I think I've got an **idea**."

Dwayne rushed off to the computer. He started work on a new flyer. I could see big, bright letters on the screen. I leaned over Dwayne's shoulder to read them.

**TOO MUCH RAIN?**
**GARDEN FLOODED?**
**GARAGE UNDER WATER?**
**CALL DWAYNE!**
**I'LL CLEAR YOUR DRAINS!**